SMALL MAMMALS

BY ELISABETH HERSCHBACH

Essential Library

An Imprint of Abdo Publishing
abdobooks.com

ABDOBOOKS.COM

Published by Abdo Publishing, a division of ABDO, PO Box 398166, Minneapolis, Minnesota 55439. Copyright © 2024 by Abdo Consulting Group, Inc. International copyrights reserved in all countries. No part of this book may be reproduced in any form without written permission from the publisher. Essential Library™ is a trademark and logo of Abdo Publishing.

Printed in the United States of America, North Mankato, Minnesota.
052023
092023

Cover Photos: Shutterstock Images (front); Jiang Hongyan/Shutterstock Images (back)
Interior Photos: Shutterstock Images, 1, 12, 19, 21, 31, 36, 45, 48, 52, 58, 60, 64, 67, 90; Eric Isselee/Shutterstock Images, 3, 4–5, 26–27, 101; Farhad Ibrahimzade/Shutterstock Images, 6; Oleg Kozlov/Shutterstock Images, 8; Szasz-Fabian Jozsef/Shutterstock Images, 14; Rita Kochmarjova/Shutterstock Images, 16; Mary Swift/Shutterstock Images, 24, 30; Raquel Vizcaino/Shutterstock Images, 29; Nenad Nedomacki/Shutterstock Images, 33; Dmytro Leschenko/Shutterstock Images, 38; Absolut Images/Shutterstock Images, 40; Marina Tr/Shutterstock Images, 42; Irina Vasilevskaia/Shutterstock Images, 43; Dmytro Gilitukha/Shutterstock Images, 50; Joni Hanebutt/Alamy, 54; Tasia Wells/Getty Images Entertainment/Getty Images, 56; Anthony Kwan/AP Images, 61; Alex Bush/Shutterstock Images, 68–69, 100; Yichuan Cao/Sipa USA/AP Images, 70; Mint Images/Shutterstock Images, 72; Michael Macor/The San Francisco Chronicle/Hearst Newspapers/Getty Images, 75; Rosa Jay/Shutterstock Images, 79; Rachata Teyparsit/Shutterstock Images, 80; Bluedog Studio/Shutterstock Images, 82; Wahyudi/AFP/Getty Images, 85; Dasril Roszandi/NurPhoto/Getty Images, 87; Dennis Attard/Shutterstock Images, 93; Daniela Baumann/Shutterstock Images, 94; Christa Boaz/iStockphoto, 97; Africa Studio/Shutterstock Images, 99

Editor: Marie Pearson
Series Designer: Becky Daum

Library of Congress Control Number: 2022948871

PUBLISHER'S CATALOGING-IN-PUBLICATION DATA
Names: Herschbach, Elisabeth, author.
Title: Small Mammals / by Elisabeth Herschbach
Description: Minneapolis, Minnesota: Abdo Publishing Company, 2024 | Series: Essential pets | Includes online resources and index.
Identifiers: ISBN 9781098290566 (lib. bdg.) | ISBN 9781098276744 (ebook)
Subjects: LCSH: Pets--Juvenile literature. | Rodents as pets--Juvenile literature. | Mammals--Juvenile literature. | Pets--Behavior--Juvenile literature. | Zoology--Juvenile literature.
Classification: DDC 636.0887--dc23

CONTENTS

SMALL MAMMALS AS PETS

Benjy the rabbit twitches his nose and hops in excited circles as Sophie approaches his enclosure with a bowl of fresh veggies. The staple of Benjy's diet is grass hay, which gives him the fiber he needs for healthy digestion and to grind down his teeth. But Sophie also feeds Benjy a variety of fresh vegetables and occasional fruit to make sure he has a balanced diet with plenty of vitamins. Today's menu includes romaine lettuce, cucumber slices, and sprigs of parsley—his favorite!

While Benjy nibbles his greens contentedly, Sophie replenishes his hay, washes and refills his water bowl, and tidies up his enclosure. Then it's exercise time. Sophie opens Benjy's enclosure and

The checkered giant is one of many breeds of rabbits.

Because rabbits can be litter box trained, they are less messy than some other small mammals when allowed to explore.

lets him out to roam the whole room. He zooms across the floor, kicking up his hind legs in lively leaps. When he needs a rest, he likes to cuddle next to Sophie as she reads or watches TV. Sophie isn't worried that Benjy will leave a mess on the floor because she has trained him to use a litter box.

Benjy is a gray-and-white rabbit Sophie adopted from the animal shelter. Sophie had seen his photo on the shelter website and fallen in love with his long, velvety ears, bright eyes, and adorable furry face. But before deciding to adopt Benjy, she spent several days researching rabbits and how to care for them. Finally, Sophie was ready to take the plunge. Taking care of Benjy would be a big responsibility, but she knew she could give him the time and attention he needed.

POPULAR PETS

In the United States in 2022, 6.2 million households owned a small mammal.[1] Rabbits are the most popular small mammals kept as pets in the United States. Their sweet nature and fluffy good looks attract many pet owners. With their cotton-ball tails and twitchy noses, rabbits are friendly, intelligent creatures that make excellent companions. But many other small mammals also make great pets.

People who like cute, furry animals but want something smaller than a dog or cat have many options

DEGUS

Close relatives of guinea pigs and chinchillas, degus began rising in popularity in the 2010s. Slightly larger than rats, with a silky gray-brown coat and a long, tufted tail, these social rodents are native to South America, where they live in the Andes Mountains. In the wild, degus live together in communal burrows. For that reason, it's always better for pet owners to get at least two degus so they can keep each other company.

Unlike many rodents, degus are awake and active during the day. This, along with their engaging personalities, makes them an appealing choice for a small pet. Degus are curious and intelligent and can be easily tamed when handled from a young age. In 2008, researchers in Japan trained degus to use a small rake to retrieve food—the first known example of rodents using tools.

Because of their activity level, degus need a cage with plenty of space, plus time outside of their cages to explore and get exercise. To stay clean, they also need regular sand baths, which help remove oils from their fur. With proper care and nutrition, these herbivores can live an average of six to nine years.[2]

to choose from. These include guinea pigs, hamsters, gerbils, mice, rats, and ferrets. A variety of more exotic small mammals are also becoming increasingly popular as pets, such as chinchillas, hedgehogs, degus, sugar gliders, and prairie dogs.

Like almost all mammals, these furry creatures are warm blooded, give birth to live young, and nurse their babies with milk from mammary glands. Compared with other mammals, they are all relatively small. Beyond these similarities, however, small mammals all have their own distinct traits and needs. From physical appearance to personality and behavior, different species vary widely.

Gerbils and mice are tiny enough to fit in the palm of a hand. Guinea pigs can grow up to one foot (0.3 m) long.[3] Hamsters are frisky and love to run, burrow, and explore, but they typically prefer not to be handled.

Rats and ferrets, by contrast, love human interaction. Chinchillas have silky, soft fur, while hedgehogs have stiff quills on their backs.

Many small mammals are nocturnal, which means they are most active at night. Others are diurnal, asleep at night and active during the daytime. Some species are very social and need to be kept in pairs, such as gerbils. Others, like hamsters, are solitary and do best alone. Even tail types differ. Gerbils, mice, and rats have long, skinny tails. Chinchilla tails are fluffy and squirrel-like. Hamsters have short tails, and guinea pigs do not have tails.

Even within a single species, there can be a great deal of variety. For example, the American Rabbit Breeders Association recognizes nearly 50 different breeds of pet rabbits, all with varying sizes, colors, and fur types.[8] Some have upright ears, while others have floppy ears. Guinea pigs also come in a range of colors, from beige to black or tortoiseshell. Some are short haired, while others are long haired.

SMALL PETS, BIG COMMITMENT

Figuring out which small mammal is a good fit takes research and thought. And owning any pet is a big commitment. Despite their size, small mammals still require a lot of attention. Caring for one properly takes time and work. But as Sophie learned from her pet rabbit, Benjy, taking care of a small mammal is a rewarding experience.

Small mammals make appealing pets for many reasons. They don't bark or meow, and they typically need less space than a dog or cat. Small pets can also be relatively easy to take care of. Abby Chronister, a graphic designer from Kansas, was struggling with anxiety and depression when she decided to get pet rats. She explained that some people may not have the energy to walk a dog often, but they may be able to care for a small mammal, which doesn't require as much physical activity on the owner's part. Most small mammals have a relatively short life span, which can be a selling point for those unable to make a longer-term commitment. And small mammals can be the perfect alternative for apartment dwellers who live in buildings that don't allow dogs or cats.

When Alice Dontanville, for example, was blocked by her lease from getting a dog, she opted for a chinchilla. "He loves your attention the same way a dog really loves human attention," she says. "It's the appeal of a puppy without the daily walks."[9]

Whatever the species, small mammal pets can be fun to spend time with. They are playful and entertaining to watch. When socialized, they are often friendly to their owners. They provide comfort and companionship. "Ferrets are beautiful creatures and so entertaining, I canceled my TV subscription," says Bonnie Russell, cofounder of a ferret rescue group in the Washington, DC, metropolitan area. And Chronister says of her pet rats, "Those little critters are what made me get out of bed, knowing I had those little lives to care for."[10]

Pet small mammals can provide owners with comfort and entertainment just like dogs or cats can.

FROM WILD TO HOUSE PETS

The history of small mammals as pets differs greatly by species. Some are still wild. People have to raise each individual animal to be tame. Taming is changing the behavior of one animal by training and exposure. Those changes can't be passed down to its offspring. Other small mammals have been domesticated. Domestication is the process of adapting animals from their wild or natural state to provide some benefit to humans, such as food, labor, or in the case of pets, companionship.

By controlling which animals reproduce together, breeders emphasize certain traits over others, producing offspring with more desired traits. This process is known as selective breeding.

The domestic mouse is descended from the wild house mouse.

Domesticated animals are easier to teach to be unafraid of humans than wild animals are.

RABBITS

Rabbits are one species that has been domesticated. Worldwide, there are 29 different species of wild rabbits.[1] Found on every continent except Antarctica, they live in many different environments—from grasslands and forests to wetlands and deserts. The wild cottontails found across North America shelter in shallow hollows scratched out in grass or in holes made by groundhogs or other animals. Other rabbit species dig underground burrows,

People have bred rabbits for certain traits. The Angora rabbit has long fur.

called warrens, where they live in extended family groups. There they raise their young, which are born blind, deaf, and helpless. At dawn and dusk, rabbits leave the safety of their nests to nibble on grass and other plants. Constantly on the alert, they rely on their keen hearing to detect potential threats. Their strong hind legs let them quickly bound away from predators.

Wild rabbits look similar to pet rabbits. They are small and soft, with the same long ears and fluffy tails as their pet counterparts. But a wild rabbit would not make a good pet. In the wild, rabbits are prey animals, so they are very nervous by nature. For that reason, they are not comfortable around humans or suited to a life in captivity. Domestic pet rabbits, by contrast, have become much less nervous.

Today's pet bunnies are descended from a species called the European wild rabbit, native to southwestern Europe. But generations of selective breeding have changed them. Their wild ancestors roamed rugged grasslands in France and Spain for thousands of years, hunted by Stone Age hunters. Invading Roman armies may have introduced them into northern Europe some 2,000 years ago. By the Middle Ages (500–1500 CE), they were widespread across Europe. Breeders started raising them in artificial warrens. These rabbits weren't pets. They were farmed for their meat and fur. Keeping rabbits as pets didn't become popular until the 1700s. That's also when selective breeding intensified.

Over time, rabbit lovers have created many different domestic breeds. Tiny dwarf varieties can weigh just two pounds (0.9 kg).[2] Giant breeds can get bigger than house cats. Shapes, colors, and fur types vary. Domestic rabbits are also less fearful and skittish than wild ones. In the wild, bold rabbits would be more likely to be eaten. But in captivity, people often breed the tamest rabbits that get along the best with people.

GUINEA PIGS

Other small mammals have also been domesticated. These include ferrets, mice, rats, and guinea pigs. The guinea pigs kept as pets no longer exist in the wild. Sometimes called cavies after their scientific name—*Cavia porcellus*—they are a domesticated species descended from rodents native to South America. Their ancestors came from the Andes Mountains where they lived in small groups in grassland habitats. There they foraged for food and burrowed in the thick grass to escape from predators.

In the 1500s, Spanish conquerors colonized South America. By this time, guinea pigs had already been domesticated for more than 5,000 years. The Inca people of South America raised them for food, often keeping them indoors in special rooms. Archaeological evidence

Owners can exercise their creativity by designing homes for their guinea pigs or other small mammals.

suggests that guinea pigs were also used in religious rituals and ceremonies. The Inca bred guinea pigs to have a larger body weight and bigger litter size than their ancestors.

The Spanish exported guinea pigs to Europe, where they became popular as household pets. As pets, they were bred for their temperament and the appearance of their fur. Today's domestic guinea pigs are less aggressive than their wild relatives would have been and get stressed less easily.

PETS WITH A PURPOSE

Ferrets belong to the weasel family, which includes badgers, polecats, ermines, minks, stoats, and wolverines. Domestic ferrets are thought to be descendants of the European polecat, native to Europe and part of Russia and North Africa. Their wild ancestors lived in lowland areas in habitats including wetlands, wooded areas, grasslands, and coastal areas. Using their keen senses, they hunted for prey at night.

The first ferrets were working animals. Ancient Greeks are thought to have bred ferrets as early as 2,500 years ago to hunt rabbits and rodents. With their narrow bodies and flexible spines, ferrets could easily squeeze down holes to root out prey. By the Middle Ages, ferrets were widely used for pest control across Europe and Asia, including by Mongolian emperor and conqueror Genghis Khan. Ships traveling to the United States in the

ON THE FAST TRACK

Compared with other popular pets, hamsters and gerbils have a relatively short history of being domesticated. Hamsters were not bred in captivity until the 1930s. They did not become popular as pets until the 1950s. Gerbils caught on as pets even later, in the 1960s. However, both hamsters and gerbils mate often and have large litters. This means many generations of animals are produced in a short amount of time, allowing breeders to make changes more quickly than in species that reproduce more slowly.

CHINCHILLAS

Chinchillas are close relatives of guinea pigs. They come from the Andes. In the wild, they live at high altitudes, where it can get very cold. Their extremely thick fur helps them survive in these temperatures. However, this plush fur also made chinchillas attractive to fur traders.

Clothing made from chinchilla fur became highly fashionable in Europe in the 1700s. A single coat would require pelts from more than 100 of the small rodents.[3] By the 1900s, chinchillas had been hunted nearly to extinction.

As a result, Argentina, Bolivia, Chile, and Peru banned the hunting of wild chinchillas. However, an American mining engineer named Mathias Chapman brought specimens back to the United States in the 1920s. He began commercially breeding them for their fur. By the 1960s, chinchillas had also become popular as pets.

Today, chinchillas are still endangered in the wild. It remains illegal to hunt or sell wild chinchillas, but habitat destruction threatens their survival. Although their numbers in the wild are dwindling, captive-bred chinchillas are commercially raised in large numbers for the fur and pet industries. Almost all pet chinchillas in the United States today are descendants of the animals Chapman originally imported.

1700s kept ferrets on board to kill rodents, and American farmers used them to ward off mice and rats infesting their barns and granaries. Because they were used as working animals, ferrets needed to be easy to handle. For that reason, they were bred to be tamer and less fearful around humans. Those traits made them attractive as pets.

In the 1500s, Queen Elizabeth I reportedly kept a pet ferret. Then in the 1800s, Queen Victoria bred ferrets to give as gifts. People breeding ferrets for pets placed special importance on a tame temperament. As a result, while their wild polecat relatives are solitary and nervous, domestic ferrets have become very social and outgoing.

FROM PEST TO PET

People have long considered mice and rats to be pests. Fossil evidence shows that mice have been living near human settlements for 15,000 years. Native to India, these tiny rodents spread across Asia and Europe as human settlements grew with the rise of agriculture. They thrived by scavenging stores of grain and food scraps. Later, European ships carried stowaway mice to other corners of the globe, where they quickly reproduced.

Rats also thrived by living alongside human settlements. From their native East Asia, they spread across the globe through human migration and trade.

Rats and mice have a high birth rate and can adapt to a
wide range of environments. This has made them some
of the world's most widespread invasive species. Wild
mice and rats can cause significant damage, including
destroying crops, contaminating food supplies, and
transmitting diseases.

Nonetheless, their reputation as pests hasn't stopped
mice and rats from becoming household pets. Domestic
varieties, known as fancy mice and rats, have enjoyed a
long history as pets. The earliest written reference to
a domestic mouse comes from an 1100 BCE Chinese
text. By the 1700s,
breeders in China and
Japan had produced
many domesticated
varieties of mice, and
the tradition of keeping
mice as pets spread
to Europe.

Domestic rats were
bred in Japan as early as
the 1600s. Rat catchers
in 1800s England
popularized the practice
of keeping them as
pets. Hired to help clean

up the rat-infested streets of London, some rat catchers made extra money on the side by taming some of the unusually colored rats they found. These people bred the rats, decorated them with ribbons, and sold them as pets. Fancy rats remain popular today. "A well-bred rat will be kind of like a well-bred dog," says Chronister. "They will be friendly. They will be curious. And they will cuddle."[4]

Pet rats come in many colors and patterns, including spotted.

WILD AT HEART

Not all animals bred in captivity are domesticated. Instead, these animals are tamed. Certain exotic pets such as sugar gliders and prairie dogs are some of the undomesticated small mammals kept as pets. Sugar gliders are small marsupials native to Australia, Indonesia, and Papua New Guinea. The winglike flaps of skin between their front and back legs enable them to glide through the air. These nocturnal animals have grown in popularity as pets in the first few decades of the 2000s. Their small size and large eyes attract many buyers. They are energetic and need a lot of space to exercise, including space to glide. They also need to be kept with other sugar gliders. In the wild, they live in small groups.

Prairie dogs also started gaining popularity in the 2000s. They need a lot of regular interaction and handling or they will be prone to biting. They live in groups, so prairie dogs should not be kept alone. They need plenty of room to burrow into bedding.

HANDLE WITH CARE

In the wild, sugar gliders live almost completely in the treetops, gliding over long distances from tree to tree. They are sensitive and prone to stress. As a result, they often do poorly in captivity. If their needs aren't adequately met, sugar gliders can become ill or even start harming themselves. Because it is very hard to replicate their natural diet in captivity, many end up malnourished.

CHOOSING A PET

Deciding to get any pet is a big undertaking. Small mammal pets are no exception. They require feeding, supervision, and cleaning. They need plenty of interaction and stimulation. And different species have their own needs, characteristics, and behaviors. Careful thought should go into deciding which, if any, small mammal will be a good fit for a person's lifestyle. "The first question is, Why are you looking for a pet and what's important to you about the role they play in your life and what things do you want to do with them?" says Lisa LaFontaine, chief executive of the Washington Humane Society.[1]

Aspiring pet owners should thoroughly research the different options and think about what each animal needs in order to have a safe and loving home. Many books are available on pet

Some small mammals, such as ferrets, need more interaction and attention than others.

ownership, and there is a wealth of information online, such as from veterinary clinics, animal sanctuaries, and clubs that form around the ownership of a certain type of animal. Consulting a veterinarian is also a good way to get information on how to care for a small mammal. So is talking to other pet owners. They can offer an inside perspective on the daily commitment required as well as a realistic view of what it's like to live with a certain pet. From average life span to space requirements, there are many factors to consider before settling on a small mammal pet.

AVERAGE LIFE SPAN

Most small mammals have short life spans. For example, mice, gerbils, and hamsters live for only about two years, and sometimes less. Pet rats will rarely make it past three. Other small mammals have longer life spans. Guinea pigs typically live for about five to seven years.[2] The average pet ferret's life span is about five to eight years, though some can live longer.[3] A pet rabbit can live anywhere from seven to 12 years.[4] In comparison, chinchillas are long lived, with an average life span of 12 to 15 years. Some chinchillas can survive for more than 20 years.[5]

Depending on the pet owner's preferences or circumstances, average life span can be a deciding factor in choosing a pet. It can be heartbreaking to bond with a

A hamster is one option for people who do not want to commit to keeping a pet for many years.

pet only to have it die a short while later. For pet owners who are not sure they can make a longer commitment, however, a short life span can be a plus.

NOCTURNAL OR NOT?

Many small mammals are nocturnal. These include hamsters, rats, mice, hedgehogs, and sugar gliders. Guinea pigs, gerbils, and degus are diurnal. Rabbits, chinchillas, and ferrets are crepuscular animals, which means they are most active at dawn and dusk.

What type of pet works best will depend on the owner's lifestyle and schedule. Pet owners who want

Nocturnal animals may make noise at night, such as running in a wheel.

to interact with their pets during the day may find that nocturnal animals are not a good match. Some, like hamsters, can become irritable and bite if handled when they are trying to sleep. Sugar gliders can get so stressed if they are disturbed that they start harming themselves.

However, for pet owners who are gone most of the day at work or school, a nocturnal or crepuscular pet might be the perfect choice. Veronica Glickenhaus, for example, longed for a furry pet, but she and her husband were typically gone for hours every day. In the end, they decided to get two pet ferrets. The ferrets spend most of the day sleeping. Then, once the couple returns home at the end of the day, their pets are alert and ready to play.

SPACE AND TIME CONSTRAINTS

Glickenhaus says their pet ferrets make wonderful companions. "They are more fun than I can possibly describe," she says. "And they're really affectionate; they like to be held in my arms while I'm watching a movie."[6] But ferrets require more space and more hands-on attention than some other small mammals. The couple installed a large, almost shoulder-high cage in their living room to house their ferrets during the daytime. When they return home, they let their ferrets out so they get plenty of exercise and interaction.

Rabbits, guinea pigs, and prairie dogs also need ample space, plenty of time outside of their cages, and a lot

In addition to needing large cages, ferrets also need a lot of toys to play with. These toys can be store bought or homemade.

of interaction. By contrast, mice, hamsters, gerbils, and hedgehogs can be kept in smaller enclosures longer and need less interaction. These smaller pets may be good options for families with less space or busy schedules. The less demanding upkeep is one of the selling points of hedgehogs, says Jennifer Crespo, who breeds them. "A hedgehog can hang out all day while you are at work, you can come home, hang out with it for a couple of hours or, you know, put it away," she explains.[7]

But no animal can be confined to a small cage and left alone all the time. Even the tiniest rodents need adequate space, care, and stimulation. And all pets require a time investment, including feeding them and cleaning their living spaces. Before deciding to bring any pet home, families need to make sure they have the time and resources to provide that routine care.

Social animals such as degus will groom, play with, and sleep with each other.

LIFE TOGETHER

Hamsters and hedgehogs are solitary creatures, and they need to be housed alone. However, many other small mammals are very social animals. For example, ferrets, guinea pigs, rabbits, mice, rats, gerbils, and prairie dogs all live in groups in the wild. As pets, they will be happiest when kept with one or more of their own kind. To avoid unwanted babies, only animals of the same sex should be housed together, unless they are spayed or neutered.

It is especially important for social animals to be kept in groups when their owners have limited time to spend with their pets. Having a companion will keep pets from becoming lonely and bored. Some, such as degus, can get depressed to the point of illness if kept in isolation.

Prospective pet owners should think carefully about the social needs of a potential pet and whether they have the resources to meet those needs. A pair of pets will need more space than a single pet. Their care will take more time, work, and money. Figuring out the best arrangement may require some research. For example, rabbits are territorial. Introducing a companion must be done gradually and properly. Rabbits housed together should be spayed and neutered. This not only prevents unwanted babies but also curbs hormones that can lead to fighting.

HOUSEHOLD ENVIRONMENT

Although many small mammals do best when they live with members of their own species, the presence of other household pets can be stressful. That's especially true in the case of larger animals such as dogs and cats. These are

natural predators of small mammals, so small mammals
are instinctively fearful of them. A plan for safe housing
is a must. Some dogs and cats can be trained to be
friendly toward smaller pets, but they should never be
left together unsupervised. And cages should be kept
in a room the dog or cat can't access when the owners
are gone.

Other parts of the household environment are also
important to consider. For example, some small mammals
have specific temperature requirements. Chinchillas, for
example, can suffer heatstroke in temperatures above
77 degrees Fahrenheit (25°C).[9] Hamsters need to be kept
at a consistent range between about 65 and 75 degrees
Fahrenheit (18–24°C).[10] Temperature requirements differ
by animal, so finding the ideal range for a specific pet will
take research.

In addition, a household that is very noisy and chaotic
can be a stressful living environment for a small mammal.
Most are easily scared. Although they have evolved to be
much calmer and tamer than their wild relatives, they still
retain some of the nervous instincts of prey animals.

Because these tiny animals are so fragile and nervous,
a household with very young children may not be a safe
environment for them. Although they are small, they
are hard to handle correctly and can be easily injured.
Some, such as hamsters and hedgehogs, may bite or

scratch when scared. Others, like guinea pigs, are unlikely to bite but can be harmed if mishandled. They often squirm when picked up, which makes them easy to drop. For that reason, it can be unsafe to let young children handle them.

NOT FOR EVERYONE

Experts say that small mammals are not appropriate pets for children younger than seven. Even for many older children, small mammals will not be a good fit. Typically, children want pets that will cuddle and readily interact. Many adult pet owners do too. Small mammals are naturally timid. It takes time and patience to win their trust and form a bond. People who don't have that patience may end up frustrated or bored with their pet.

When an owner buys a small mammal on a whim or with misperceptions about how much care it will take, and that pet doesn't meet the owner's desires, the pet often ends up abandoned. This is especially a problem for rabbits around Easter time. Every year, sales of pet bunnies spike in the weeks leading up to Easter. Once the novelty wears off, large numbers of those impulse purchases end up abandoned. Many are let loose in the wild, even though domestic rabbits lack the skills needed to survive outdoors. Others are taken to shelters, which struggle to keep up with the influx in the following month.

Jennifer McGee, comanager of a southeastern Georgia shelter, says calls from people trying to unload their unwanted pet rabbits average three to four a day in the six weeks after Easter. That compares with only one or two calls a week during the rest of the year.[11] "No animal should be an impulse buy," says Vineeta Anand, founder of the Virginia-based organization Friends of Rabbits.[12]

CHAPTER 4

SMALL MAMMAL CARE

Choosing the right pet takes careful research. Knowing how to properly care for a pet takes research too. According to veterinarian Gary Weitzman, the main reason rabbits end up in shelters is that people don't know how to care for them. The situation is similar with other small mammal pets. Because they are so small, they are often marketed as easy starter pets. "I think people don't think about the care of small animals," says Katheryn Collins, who rescues gerbils, hamsters, and mice. "They just think, 'I'll just get a small cage.'"[1]

However, small mammals can be challenging to care for. They are sensitive, with complex needs. Many have very particular requirements,

Each small mammal species has unique care requirements, from diet to exercise and housing.

Guinea pigs should get a variety of leafy greens and vegetables when they are young. Adults are less likely to be willing to try new foods.

including specialized diets. Like all pets, small mammals need proper nutrition and a clean, safe place to live. To stay healthy, they need adequate exercise and stimulation. But the details of their care and nutrition will vary from species to species. That is why it is always important to seek expert advice and follow recommended guidelines for the specific animal.

NUTRITION

All small mammal pets need fresh water daily and a balanced diet. For rabbits and guinea pigs, that means a strictly plant-based diet. These herbivores need plenty of hay plus fresh greens and other vegetables daily. Vegetables high in vitamin C are especially important for guinea pigs. They are one of only three animal species whose bodies cannot manufacture vitamin C, with the other two being humans and marmosets. For that reason, guinea pig diets must include plenty of this essential vitamin. Good sources include broccoli, spinach, dandelion leaves, kale, watercress, and arugula. Veterinarians often recommend a vitamin C supplement as well, given in liquid or tablet form.

Though chinchillas are also herbivores, many common vegetables are unsafe for them. Others they can tolerate only in small amounts. Because chinchillas have such sensitive stomachs, experts typically recommend feeding them specially formulated, commercially available chinchilla pellets, along with hay. Store-bought pellets are also recommended for degus, along with leafy greens and ample hay. Care must be taken never to give degus sweet foods, including fruit. They are highly prone to diabetes.

In comparison with herbivores, small mammals that are not strictly vegetarian need a diet lower in fiber and higher in protein. Mice, rats, hamsters, gerbils, hedgehogs, and ferrets fall in this category. In the wild, mice, rats, hamsters, and gerbils eat grains, seeds, and other plant matter, as well as worms, insects, and other sources of animal protein. In captivity, these omnivores are typically fed a mixture of seeds, grains, store-bought pellets, and small amounts of fresh fruits and vegetables.

Insects make up the bulk of a hedgehog's diet in the wild, but they also eat some plants and even the occasional baby mouse. Pet hedgehogs can be fed specially formulated hedgehog pellets. As a supplement two to three times a week, they can be given insects, such as mealworms and crickets, along with fresh fruits and vegetables or hard-boiled eggs.[2]

Ferrets are exclusively carnivores. In the wild, their relatives eat rabbits and rodents. For pet ferrets, commercially made ferret food is available in kibble form. Many pet owners choose to feed their ferrets

Cockroaches raised for food are among the insects a hedgehog can eat.

Ferrets can enjoy quail eggs as part of their diet.

store-bought food, with occasional supplements such as bonemeal and eggs. Some opt for a homemade diet, which includes raw or cooked meat and organs and raw bones or a replacement supplement. Any homemade diet must be based on careful research and crafted with the help of an animal nutritionist who is familiar with ferrets. In addition, the US Centers for Disease Control and Prevention (CDC) warns that raw food can harbor deadly bacteria. To minimize the risk of contamination, raw food must always be handled with care, and a thorough cleaning of surfaces and bowls must be done after each feeding.

LIVING SPACES

Most small mammal pets are kept in cages or other enclosures for at least some of the time. One important factor in selecting an appropriate enclosure is size. "Being prepared to invest a little bit into big enough caging is important in providing the animal with a decent home," says Alice Blue-McLendon, a clinical associate professor at the Texas A&M College of Veterinary Medicine & Biomedical Sciences.[3] The right dimensions vary depending on an animal's size and habits, but all small mammals need an adequate amount of space to thrive.

For guinea pigs, that means at least eight square feet (0.7 sq m) of living space per animal.[4] Rabbits need a space at least four times as long as their bodies.[5] This usually works out to a minimum of 12 square feet (1 sq m) for each rabbit.[6] Rats need at least two square feet (0.2 sq m) to themselves. "Depending on how many rats you have, that need for space can quickly add up," says Sarah Armstrong, who has four pet rats.[7] She houses them in a four-level cage that is taller than her.

Because they are so small, mice, gerbils, and hamsters can be kept in smaller spaces, such as an aquarium tank with a lid. Cages with bars, however, offer better ventilation and may be easier to clean. Some cages come with multiple levels, and a variety of add-on tubes and tunnels are available to provide climbing opportunities.

Many of the cages sold in pet shops are too small, warns Weitzman. "When buying a habitat for your pet, bigger is always better and there is no such thing as too big," he says.[8] In order to provide a large enough space, some pet owners opt for other types of enclosures instead of cages. For example, large exercise pens marketed for dogs can work well as habitats for some animals, including rabbits and guinea pigs. These portable pens are made up of wire panels that connect together and can be stretched

Rats need a lot of toys and things to interact with to keep from getting bored.

out into different shapes, forming an enclosed area.

In addition to size, another factor to keep in mind when selecting a pet's enclosure is the material. For animals that chew a lot, such as rats and chinchillas, metal cages work better than plastic or wood so they can't chew their way out. For wire cages, proper spacing of the bars is also crucial. If the spacing between bars is too wide, pets can squeeze through or get stuck. And the bottom of the cage should always be solid, rather than wire flooring, which hurts their feet.

COMFY AND CLEAN

Inside their living space, small mammals need a hiding place, such as a nesting box, plus a layer of soft bedding lining the bottom of the enclosure. Burrowers such as mice, rats, gerbils, and hamsters need a particularly deep layer of bedding to tunnel down in. For bedding, shredded dye-free paper or wood shavings are commonly used. Shavings made from cedar or pine are to be avoided, however, since the scent can be toxic for many small mammals. Likewise, sawdust and straw are not considered appropriate bedding materials. The fine flakes of sawdust can irritate pets' eyes, and straw can have sharp ends. For guinea pigs and rabbits, another option is to line their enclosure with blankets, washing them frequently.

Small mammals are naturally very clean animals. They groom themselves regularly, and many designate a specific space in their enclosure to use as their bathroom. But just as human houses need regular cleaning, so do these pets' living spaces. A dirty environment is unhygienic for small mammals, so keeping their living spaces in good shape is crucial for their health. Each day, any uneaten food or soiled bedding should be removed. At least

LITTER BOX TRAINING

In addition to rabbits, ferrets and rats can also be taught to use a litter box. Their natural preference for going to the bathroom in one spot makes them relatively easy to train. Litter box training makes it easier to give these animals a lot of cage-free time, since the risk of accidents is minimized. As with bedding, it is important to choose the right kind of litter. Some kinds are not safe for them, including the clumping types used for cats.

once a week, their enclosures should be more thoroughly cleaned. The bedding should be completely changed and surfaces should be cleaned with soap and water. Some small mammals, including mice and rats, produce a lot of smelly urine. If not properly cleaned, their cages will smell unpleasant. Their cages may need to be cleaned more often than others. Meanwhile, gerbils and degus produce very little urine.

EXERCISE AND ENRICHMENT

No matter how clean and comfortable its cage is, an animal will get bored and restless without adequate

Hiding food in food puzzles can encourage small mammals of any species to problem solve.

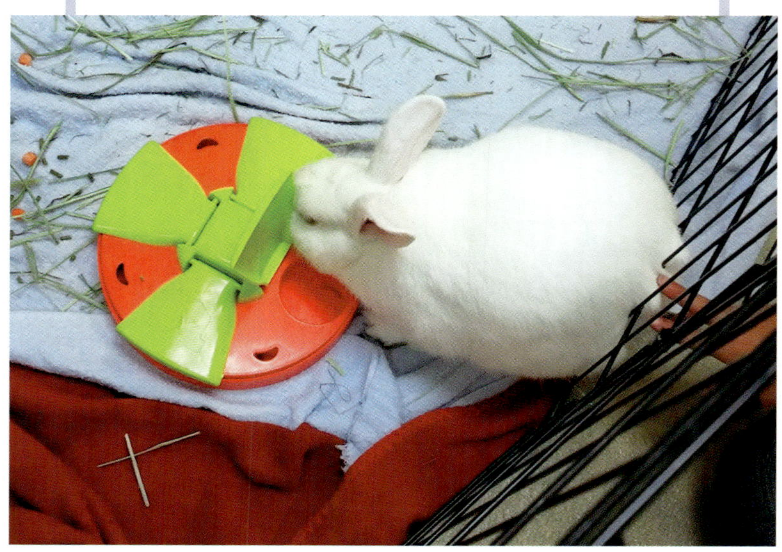

opportunities for exercise and enrichment. Hamsters, mice, gerbils, and rats can exercise in their cages on an exercise wheel. Small empty cardboard boxes and tubes make good places for them to climb and crawl through. Other toys, such as wooden chew blocks, rope ladders, ramps, balls, and tubes, can be purchased from pet stores. Stores sometimes sell tubes or exercise wheels that are too small, says Collins, so check carefully before giving them to a pet. Running in a wheel that is too small can cause the animal back problems.

All small mammal pets benefit from time outside of their cages to exercise and explore. Mice, gerbils, and hamsters are easy to lose track of in a room. These tiny, agile creatures can quickly disappear out of sight or slip into small spaces. Setting up a contained area such as a playpen can be a good way to allow them to safely roam outside of their cages. New pets need time to adjust to their home and owner before being let out.

For bigger and more active animals, plenty of time outside their cages is a must. A ferret needs at least two to three hours outside of its cage every day, but preferably more.[9] This is also true of rabbits. Guinea pigs and rats should also be given considerable cage-free time. Any room or area they are allowed to explore must be carefully pet proofed. That means making sure there are no poisonous plants within reach, putting electrical

cords out of reach or encasing them in plastic to make them chew proof, and blocking any holes, cracks, or small spaces that a pet might crawl into and get stuck in. Even if the space seems safe, small mammals should never be left out of their cages unsupervised. "It's like having a two-year-old. You have to watch them constantly or they get into trouble," says ferret rescuer Bonnie Russell.[10]

HEALTH CARE

Like their bigger counterparts, small pets also need regular health care. Ideally, they should be seen by vets who specialize in treating small mammals. Vets with this expertise are not as common as vets who treat dogs and cats. As a result, health care for small mammals tends to be expensive.

SPECIAL NEEDS

Different pets need different routine care. Both chinchillas and degus need a weekly dust or sand bath to clean their fur of naturally occurring oils. While rats, mice, gerbils, and hamsters usually wear down their own nails through activity, ferrets, rabbits, and guinea pigs need their nails regularly trimmed. Rabbits and rodents normally grind down their teeth by gnawing, but some animals have misaligned teeth. Their teeth have to be trimmed by the vet to keep them from overgrowing.

Ferrets can be taken for walks on a leash and harness.

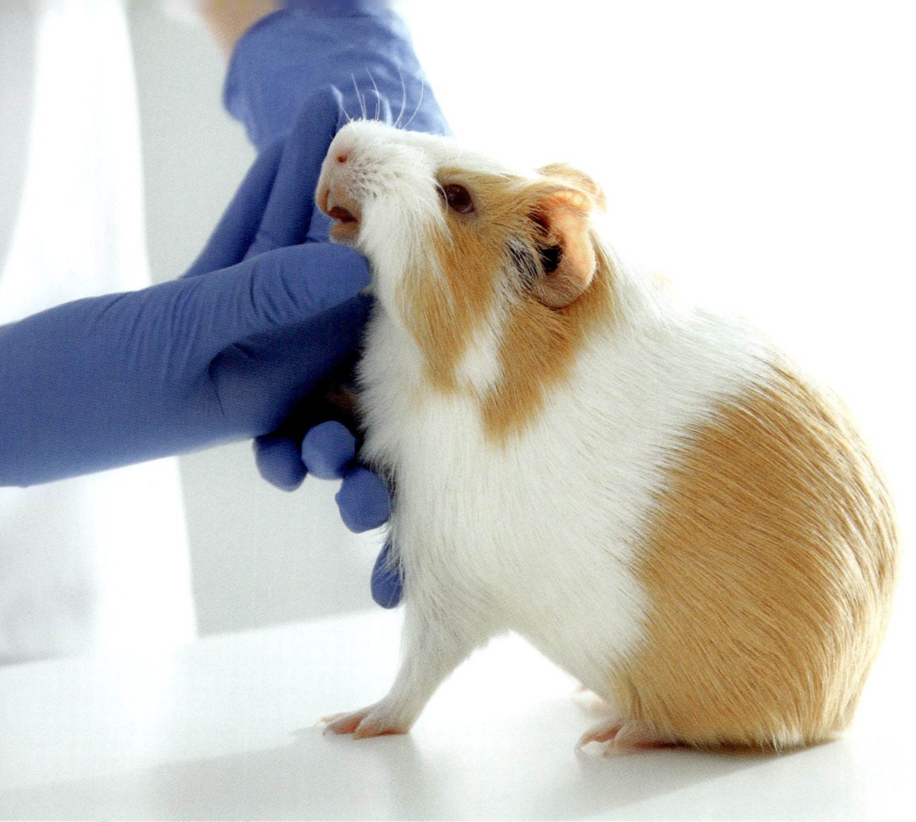

Small mammals are considered exotic animals. People can find vets specializing in exotic companion animals through the American Animal Hospital Association or the Association of Exotic Mammal Veterinarians.

Veterinarians recommend that all small mammals get routine checkups to monitor their health. Right after a pet is adopted is the most important time for a checkup. At this first visit, the vet will discuss proper nutrition, housing, handling, and care. They will check a pet's overall health, and they will offer advice on how to monitor a pet for potential signs of poor health. These include changes in activity level or appetite, hunched posture, discharge from the eyes or nose, diarrhea, and bare patches of fur.

When properly cared for, small mammals are generally hardy, healthy creatures. However, their small size makes them delicate, so when they do become ill, their health can quickly take a turn for the worse. Regularly handling a pet and interacting with it will help an owner pick up on signs of illness. And regular vet visits can help spot a disease before it becomes too serious.

In addition to routine checkups, vets recommend that rabbits and ferrets be spayed or neutered—even if they are not around the opposite sex. Spaying and neutering can protect these animals against certain cancers they are prone to. Getting a rabbit spayed or neutered also helps reduce hormone-driven behaviors that can emerge in adolescent rabbits. Neutering a male ferret will reduce the strong, musky smell it naturally gives off.

Vaccination needs depend on the species. Rats and other small rodents don't have approved vaccines. Ferrets require a series of vaccinations against distemper, a contagious viral disease that attacks their respiratory, gastrointestinal, and nervous systems. They should also be vaccinated against rabies, a viral disease that attacks the central nervous system. Rabies can also spread to and kill humans. Currently the only vaccine approved for rabbits in the United States is for rabbit hemorrhagic disease virus, a lethal viral disease that attacks a rabbit's liver.

ALL LIVING THINGS
Market MEDLEY
TROPICAL-FLAVORED DROPS
Ideal for Rabbits, Guinea Pigs, Hamsters & Other Small Animals
Gâteries Pour Petits Animaux
SMALL PET TREAT With Real Fruit
ALL LIVING THINGS
ALT MM YUM DROP TRPICAL TREATS 4 OZ (C)
12/02/19
*1.13
UNIT PRICE PER OZ
4 49
73725779749
5283232
NET WT 3 OZ

ALL LIVING THINGS
Market MEDLEY
PEAS & CARROTS
Ideal for Rabbits, Guinea Pigs, Hamsters & Other Small Animals
Gâteries Pour Petits Animaux
Real VEGETABLES
NET WT 3 OZ (85 g)
RESEAL FOR FRESHNESS
3 69
73725779444
5283084

ALL LIVING THINGS
Market MEDLEY
GARDEN TREATS
Ideal for Rabbits, Guinea Pigs, Hamsters Mice & Other Small Animals
Gâteries Pour Petits Animaux
MADE WITH Real Carrots & Real
RESEAL FOR FRESHNESS
MADE WITH Real Papaya

ALL LIVING THINGS
ALT MM FRUIT BLEND TREATS, 3.5 OZ (C)
12/02/19
*1.14
UNIT PRICE PER OZ
3 99
73725779740
5283225
3.5 OZ

ALL LIVING THINGS
ALT MM BERRY TREATS 1 OZ (C)
12/02/19
*1.13
UNIT PRICE PER OZ
4 49
73725779741
5283226

ALL LIVING THINGS
ALT MM SHORTBREAD SNACK TREATS .3OZ (C)
12/02/19
*1.33
UNIT PRICE PER OZ
3 99
73725779748
5283233

Market MEDLEY
SHORTBREAD SNACKS
Ideal for Rabbits, Guinea Pigs, Hamsters & Other Small Animals
Gâteries Pour Petits Animaux
LIVING THINGS
RESEAL FOR FRESHNESS

Market MEDLEY
FRUITY MIX
Ideal for Rabbits, Guinea Pigs, Hamsters & Other Small Animals
Gâteries Pour Petits Animaux
MADE WITH Real Fruit
LIVING THINGS
RESEAL FOR FRESHNESS

Market MEDLEY
BERRY-FLAVORED DROPS
Ideal for Rabbits, Guinea Pigs, Hamsters & Other Small Animals
Small Pet TREAT
NET WT 4 OZ
ALL LIVING THINGS
RESEAL FOR FRESHNESS

BROWN'S
Tropical Carnival
GOURMET TREATS
Farm Fresh FIXINS Treats
For Rabbits, Guinea Pigs, Other Small Animals

TROPICAL CARNIVAL
TROPICAL CARNIVAL FARM FRSH TREATS (C)
12/02/19
58¢
UNIT PRICE PER OZ
5 79
18 OZ
04293444947
5175719

ALL LIVING THINGS
ALT MM MIXED BLEND TREATS, 2.5 OZ (C)
12/02/19
*1.48
UNIT PRICE PER OZ
3 69
2.5 OZ
73725779743
5283228

ALL LIVING THINGS
Market MEDLEY
MIXED TREATS
Ideal for Rabbits, Guinea Pigs, Hamsters & Other Small Animals
Gâteries Pour Petits Animaux
Small Pet TREAT
RESEAL FOR FRESHNESS

INDUSTRY AND COMMUNITY

The typical retail cost of a small mammal pet tends to be low. For example, pet mice usually cost less than $10.[1] However, once supplies and upkeep are factored in, the costs add up quickly. For pet owners like Sarah Armstrong, the expense is worth it. "When I come home to see my rats all waiting to give me snuffly little kisses, I couldn't imagine a more perfect pet," she says about her four rats.[2] But not everyone can make the same commitment, and some animals will cost more than others.

So before choosing a pet, it's important to have a realistic view of the costs and a financial plan for covering them. "Look at your environment and financial status to make sure you have a budget in mind," says veterinarian Chris Miller. "Take into account what each species or breed brings with it as far as dietary and

Pet stores sell many of the items small mammal owners need, from food to toys and cages.

medical needs."[3] After preparing a budget and doing plenty of research, it's time to get the pet.

WHERE TO GET A PET

Shelters and rescue organizations are full of pets in need of a good home. That's why many animal advocates urge would-be pet owners to first check with a local shelter or rescue. Shelters are often run by local governments. At some, unadopted animals get killed if they aren't adopted in a certain amount of time. Others are no-kill shelters, which don't euthanize animals due to lack of space, but this limits the number of animals they can take in.

Some rescues hold fundraising events where people can enter their pets in competitions and also meet adoptable small mammals.

Rescue groups are usually private, nonprofit organizations. They place abandoned animals in foster homes until permanent homes can be found. Many rescue groups specialize in a specific animal, whereas shelters take in a mix of animals. Both shelters and rescues charge a small adoption fee, which helps fund their continued operation. Available animals can range from young to senior in age. Prospective adopters should carefully screen a rescue or shelter to make sure it is responsible. A few rescues hoard animals and mistreat them in other ways.

The rabbit rescue Peacebunny in Minnesota was charged with animal cruelty in 2022 when investigators found 47 dead rabbits and several rabbits with injuries in the facility.[4] A responsible rescue or shelter will give its animals the veterinary care they need. They should never take in more animals than they have the resources to care for. Both should carefully screen applicants to make sure they are fully committed to taking good care of their new pet.

If it's not possible to find the right pet at a local shelter or rescue group, another option is to buy a pet from a private breeder. For those looking for a specific breed or a more unusual species, a breeder is likely to be the best source. Potential buyers can find lists of registered breeders through breeder associations, such as the American Fancy Rat and Mouse Association, the American

Cavy Breeders Association, and the American Rabbit Breeders Association.

However, it is always important to carefully assess any breeder before buying a pet. While there are many reputable breeders, there are also some who do not have the animals' best interests in mind. For that reason, it is ideal to choose a local breeder and schedule an in-person visit to check out the facility. Prospective buyers should look for a clean environment and animals that are healthy and well cared for. And they should come prepared to ask lots of questions, determining whether the animals are kept in large enough cages, given opportunities to exercise, and allowed out of their cages sometimes.

Pet stores are a third option for finding a pet. Hamsters, gerbils, mice, rats, and guinea pigs are all easy to find at a local pet store, where they are marketed as pocket pets. However, not all pet stores maintain ethical standards. Some stores sell pets that are sick or keep animals in poor conditions. For example, a 2019 police investigation of a former Petland store in Fairfax, Virginia, uncovered 31 dead rabbits in a freezer.[5]

In addition, most animals sold in pet stores come from big suppliers known as pet mills. These are large-scale commercial breeders where poor treatment of animals is a widespread problem. One of many cases that have come to light involved a Pennsylvania company that supplied guinea pigs, chinchillas, hamsters, gerbils, and other rodents to pet stores nationwide. When federal investigators visited in 2019, they found unsanitary conditions and dozens of animals needing veterinary treatment.

Such cases have inspired a growing campaign to discourage people from buying animals from pet stores. Many animal advocates argue that it's the only way to put an end to unethical practices in the pet industry. Others simply say to exercise caution at pet stores. That includes checking to make sure the animals at a store look healthy and are kept in adequate conditions. It also includes finding out where a pet store gets its animals from and making sure the breeder or supplier treats them humanely.

RABBITS IN HONG KONG

Hong Kong is a densely populated city, with more than 17,000 people per square mile.[6] Most people live in apartments, and it can be challenging to own large, active pets like dogs who need a lot of exercise. Because of these space limitations, many people in Hong Kong keep smaller animals, including rabbits.

Many rabbit owners in Hong Kong love to give their pets the best they can offer. One option available to pet rabbits in the city is a luxury rabbit resort called Bunny Style. Owner Donna Li first started her business with a room for rabbits to play in. Hong Kong is very hot for much of the year, and this play area would be a comfortable temperature for the rabbits.

Now the resort offers boarding while owners travel. Resort workers will brush the rabbits and trim their nails. The rabbits can exercise in a play area. And owners can purchase cakes for their rabbits to eat. Made of grass and other

Bunny Style has play areas where boarding rabbits can exercise.

rabbit-safe foods, these cakes are shaped into flowers or tarts.

Sometimes owners can no longer keep their rabbits. Hong Kong has shelters and organizations such as Tolobunny and the Hong Kong Rabbit Society that will take in abandoned pets and help them find new homes. They also work to educate people in Hong Kong about rabbit ownership.

SUPPLIES AND EXPENSES

In general, buying a pet from a private breeder is more expensive than adopting one or buying one from a pet shop. The breed also plays a role in a pet's price. For example, most rabbits sell for about $20 to $40 at a pet store. A purebred rabbit from a show breeder, however, can cost $100.[7]

Along with the pet itself comes the upfront cost of all the initial supplies needed to properly house and care for it. These include a spacious cage or other enclosure, plus food, bedding, and accessories for feeding, drinking, and exercising. The cost of a living space varies widely by size and quality. Smaller, simpler cages for mice, hamsters, and gerbils can cost $50. Bigger, more elaborate cages suitable for larger pets like rabbits and ferrets can cost more than $200.[8] Exercise pens tend to be less expensive than cages, in addition to being more spacious and easier to clean.

For a rabbit, all these initial supplies can add up to more than $300 in addition to the cost of spaying or neutering.[9] New hamster owners should budget up to $200 for initial supplies.[10] Start-up costs for a new guinea pig will be in the same range. In addition to this initial investment, pet owners also need to budget for the ongoing costs of upkeep. These include fresh supplies of food, hay, bedding, and other essentials, plus veterinary care. "Veterinary bills alone can be several hundred dollars a year," says Vineeta Anand.[11]

Food for small mammals is not especially expensive. For example, a month's supply of hamster pellets will average between $5 and $10.[12] Quality kibble for a ferret can cost roughly $10 to $15 a month.[13] Over the course of a year, however, all the supplies needed to keep a pet healthy and happy add up quickly. All these costs will go up for pairs of pets.

To cut costs, pet owners can look for deals on food and supplies. For example, bulk food is cheaper to buy than packaged food. Hay from a local farmer will cost less than hay bought from a store. Armstrong saved money by finding a good deal on her rats' four-story cage. She also avoids pricey accessories such as store-bought toys and uses pet insurance for medical expenses. "I use CareCredit for their vet bills and budget for their needs," she says. "I buy Oxbow pellets in bulk so I save on food,

use fleece as bedding so I save on bedding, and make toys for my rats."[14]

RESOURCES FOR PET OWNERS

Organizations for pet enthusiasts are an excellent source of information for prospective pet owners. The House Rabbit Society, for example, is a nonprofit rabbit advocacy organization with chapters around the country and world. Its website includes lists of resources for rabbit owners plus tips on rabbit care, such as litter box training and rabbit proofing the home. Through the organization, rabbit lovers can also find information about how to adopt a rabbit as well as opportunities for volunteering at a shelter or fostering rabbits.

Similar organizations abound for other types of small mammals as well. For example, the American Ferret Association's website includes extensive information on caring for ferrets, including common health problems and vaccine requirements. Gerbil enthusiasts can find a detailed care guide on the American Gerbil Society website. These organizations also provide resources for finding breeders. And for pet owners interested in exploring the world of competitions and shows, they offer in-depth information on how to get involved.

PET SHOWS AND COMPETITIONS

Spending time at home with a small pet is plenty of fun. But for pet owners looking to get involved in more organized activities, there are many opportunities. Animal shows are one popular option. These shows are like beauty contests for pets. Pets are judged according to their specific breed and are evaluated on how well they compare with the ideal standard for that breed. Judges look at their fur, eyes, and overall condition, as well as their colors, markings, and other physical characteristics. "It's a lot of fun," says Jan Thomas Silva, who breeds and shows rabbits and guinea pigs. "There is great camaraderie. Everyone is usually just as excited for the winner as the winner is when he or she wins an award."[15]

There are shows for most small mammal pets, from rabbits, guinea pigs, and ferrets to hamsters, gerbils, rats, and mice. And pet owners interested in exhibiting their animals can find opportunities at the local, regional, and even national levels. However, those who decide to show will need to be selective about where they get their pets. Pets entered in animal shows need to be purchased from

For agility and hopping contests, rabbits first learn to jump low bars. Then the bars get higher as the rabbits advance.

a breeder and have a pedigree, which is a chart showing their ancestors.

In addition to pet shows that judge animals based on their breed, there are also a variety of other fun competitions, including agility contests and races. In rabbit hopping contests, for example, rabbits and their owners compete while running over jumps and navigating various obstacles on a course. For ferrets, there are tube races, yawning contests, paper bag escapes, and other fun events. There are even agility contests for gerbils. The tiny rodents navigate around obstacles as they race to the end of a course. "Anyone can buy a $12 gerbil and get into the sport of gerbil showing or gerbil agility," says Donna Anastasi, president of the American Gerbil Society. "It's very fun . . . easy and affordable."[16]

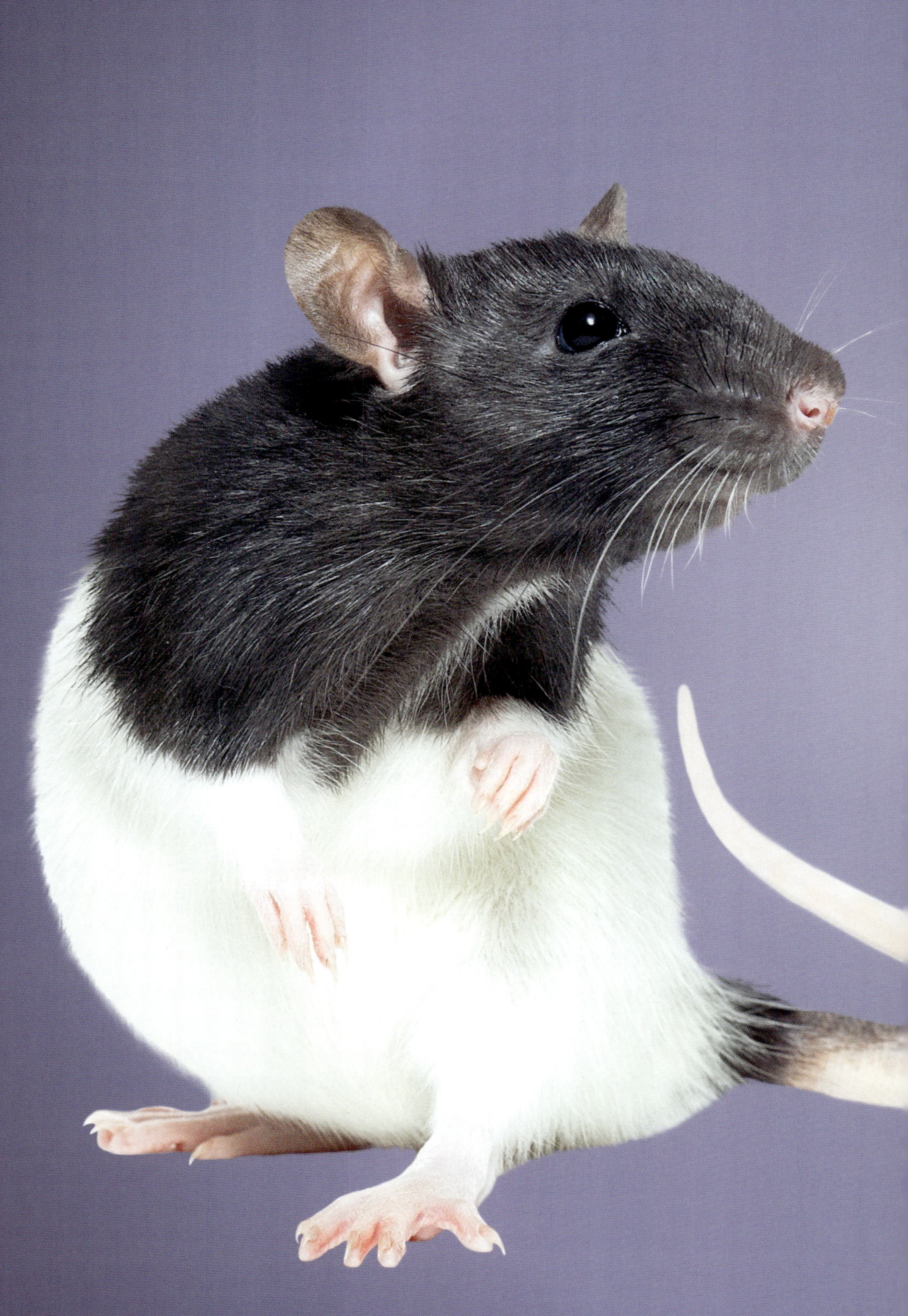

REGULATIONS

In 2016, US Department of Agriculture officials found dozens of dead and diseased small mammals in dirty and crowded conditions at Holmes Farm in Pennsylvania. The dealer was charged with more than two dozen counts of animal cruelty. Commercial breeders like Holmes Farm are federally regulated under the Animal Welfare Act (AWA). First passed in 1966, the AWA was originally enacted to regulate the breeding and treatment of animals used in research. Since then, the AWA has been amended several times. Now, it also applies to breeders and dealers who commercially supply animals as pets.

The AWA sets minimum standards for the handling, care, treatment, and transportation of animals. Critics, however, argue that the required standards are too weak, the penalties are inadequate, and enforcement is lax. In addition, the AWA's regulations do not apply to pet stores.

Some laws and regulations help protect the physical health of captive animals.

These shortcomings allow too many animal abuses to go unchecked, critics say.

PET STORE BANS

While there are no federal laws regulating pet stores, some states and cities regulate them on a local level. Some restrict where stores can get the pets they sell, requiring them to use only licensed breeders who don't have a record of certain violations.

Some have taken it a step further, banning pet stores from selling certain kinds of animals. In 2017, California became the first state to ban the sale of dogs, cats, and

Pet stores are typically allowed to sell most small companion mammals.

rabbits in pet stores. Hundreds of cities nationwide have also passed pet store bans. In most cases, these bans apply only to dogs and cats. In some municipalities, stores are also prohibited from selling rabbits. However, other types of small mammals, including hamsters, gerbils, mice, and guinea pigs, continue to be sold in large numbers in pet stores.

One exception is Cambridge, Massachusetts. There, the city council passed a law prohibiting pet shops from selling any animals unless they come from a shelter or rescue organization. That includes all small mammals. Advocates say it's important to stop financially supporting the large-scale breeders that supply pet stores and all too often keep their animals in poor conditions. "The pet shop industry cannot and has not been able to weed out bad breeders, and they do business with bad breeders, and I can't turn a blind eye to that," says Cambridge vice mayor Marc McGovern.[1]

Retail bans also aim to limit impulse buying and reduce the number of abandoned pets. One in four people surrendering a small pet to Massachusetts Society for the Prevention of Cruelty to Animals adoption centers had purchased the animal from a pet store.[2] Cities nationwide face the same problem. Some are stretched especially thin by a certain species, such as rabbits. Overburdened shelters struggle to keep up.

Pet buyers must make sure the species they want is legal in their state before purchasing an animal. Species are typically banned for human health reasons or because they could become an invasive species.

ILLEGAL PETS

Retail bans don't prevent people from owning pets. In areas with retail bans, pet stores are encouraged to team up with shelters and rescue groups to offer in-store adoption programs. In addition, these bans do not prohibit people from purchasing pets directly from responsible breeders. In some states and cities, however, owning certain pets is illegal for other reasons. So before deciding on a small mammal, prospective pet owners need to carefully check local laws.

When there are legal restrictions on owning certain pets, it is often because they are considered a possible public health risk, a potentially invasive species, or both. An invasive species is an animal that is not native to a particular ecosystem and that can cause harm to the local environment. Invasive species can be an ecological threat by competing with native wildlife for food and habitat, disrupting the balance of an ecosystem, and damaging natural resources such as crops and forests. Invasive species can also spread viruses and bacteria to native wildlife, which lacks immunity. In turn, those diseases can spread to humans. Roughly 70 percent of new infectious diseases are zoonotic, which means they originated in wildlife.[3] That includes diseases such as human immunodeficiency virus (HIV), Ebola, severe acute respiratory syndrome (SARS), and the avian flu.

Species that have only recently become popular as pets are more likely to be restricted. For example, it's illegal to keep a pet hedgehog in several states, including Georgia, California, Hawaii, and Pennsylvania. Those states consider hedgehogs a threat to local ecosystems if they escape or owners release them into the wild. In addition, the prickly insectivores can carry disease-causing bacteria such as salmonella. Similarly, pet sugar gliders are illegal in Alaska, Hawaii, and California. Degus are banned in Alaska, California, Connecticut, Georgia, and Utah.

However, even some very common household pets are restricted in certain states. For example, pet hamsters and gerbils are banned in Hawaii. That is because the natural habitat of these non-native rodents is very similar to the local climate. If they escape or are released outside, they could establish wild colonies, outcompete native species, and damage vegetation by overforaging. Gerbils are illegal to own as pets in California for the same reason.

Pet ferrets were banned in California in the 1930s, when agriculture officials warned that ferrets on the loose could endanger crops and prey on small animals such as chickens and rabbits. Since then, ferret fans have lobbied

Ferret enthusiasts have been trying to overturn California's ferret ban for decades.

extensively to try to get the ban overturned. Those who violate the ban risk six months in jail and a fine of up to $1,000 if prosecuted.[4]

Proponents of the ban cite not just the potential environmental impact of ferrets but also health concerns. Ferrets can spread rabies. Some bite and cause injury to humans. But ferret advocates argue that these concerns are overblown. A vaccinated ferret is unlikely to spread rabies. And these domesticated pets don't have the survival skills to be a threat in the wild, they say. "People think these guys will escape and form feral colonies and endanger wildlife, but they can't make it three days out on their own," says Barbara Bullock, who lives with her pet ferret Olivia in Washington, DC.[5]

San Diego resident Pat Wright agrees. The founder of LegalizeFerrets.org, a nonprofit organization, Wright has been fighting to overturn California's ban for decades. He has collected thousands of petition signatures, lobbied legislators, organized rallies, and even run for office. Despite the ban, he also keeps four ferrets. "How anyone can see these pets as a threat is absurd," he says.[6] However, one of his ferrets bit a four-year-old girl during a legalization rally. Another one bit a TV cameraman at a different rally.

THINK LOCAL

Even if a pet is legal in a state, sometimes a permit or license is required. For that reason, it is important to check the regulations before deciding to buy or adopt a pet. That includes researching local laws carefully. Some cities restrict certain pets at the local level even though there is no state-level ban. For example, although there is no state-level ban on ferrets in New York State, keeping them as pets is prohibited in New York City. Ferrets are also illegal in a handful of other cities, including Dallas, Texas, and Columbia, Missouri. Similarly, sugar gliders are banned at the city level in New York City and Saint Paul, Minnesota. Keeping a pet hedgehog is prohibited in all five boroughs of New York City and in Washington, DC.

Pet seekers should check their city's animal control ordinances for the latest information and keep in mind that regulations can change over time. For example, after being banned for 36 years in Washington, DC, pet ferrets became legal in the city in 2018. And while keeping pet prairie dogs is now legal in most states, they were banned nationwide from 2003 to 2008 after being implicated in an mpox, or monkeypox, outbreak.

KEEPING IT WILD

States and cities also have laws applying to animals removed from the wild. That's becoming increasingly important because keeping wild animals as pets is a growing trend. This is thanks in part to the influence of social media.

Nancy Coyne, a wildlife rehabilitation specialist from New York, says she often gets calls from people who bought a wild rabbit, raccoon, or other animal on a whim because they saw one kept as a pet on social media. All too often they don't realize how hard it is to care for the animal. Coyne says wild animals do not thrive in a captive environment surrounded by people. The result is a situation that is harmful for both the animals and the humans. "When they're little, they're cute and cuddly, and it starts out great," Coyne says. "Then they become aggressive and very destructive."[8]

Every state has some laws regulating the capture, keeping, or trading of wild animals. These laws are in place not just to protect wildlife but also to protect humans. In many states, it is illegal to remove an animal from the wild for use as a pet. Some allow wild animals to be kept as pets but require a special permit or license. Specific laws

Even if wild animals, such as fennec foxes, can be kept as pets with a permit, many are destructive and difficult or impossible to house train.

vary by state. For example, California and New York have strict wildlife laws. By contrast, in Arkansas a household is allowed to keep up to six wild animals without a permit.

Wild animals are also protected by legislation on both the national and international levels. The Lacey Act, enacted by the US Congress in 1900, bans illegal wildlife trafficking, or trade in animals or plants that have been illegally taken or transported from the wild. On an international level, wildlife trade is regulated by various treaties and conventions. These include the United Nations Convention on International Trade in Endangered Species of Wild Fauna and Flora (CITES), a global agreement to prevent unauthorized trade of protected species of wildlife.

CHAPTER 7

PET DEBATES

Rosie and Winnie are pet sugar gliders in New Jersey with 2.8 million followers on TikTok.[1] Maya the fennec fox, a tiny species of fox from the Sahara desert, has more than 18,000 followers on Instagram.[2] These small mammals are part of a popular trend on social media. Viral photos and videos depict a range of unusual pets, from small primates such as pygmy marmosets and squirrel monkeys to kinkajous, a tropical tree-dwelling mammal from the rain forests of South America.

These social media postings are fueling a growing demand for exotic pets—nontraditional pets that do not have an extensive history of domestication or life in captivity. This growing demand has turned the international pet trade into a booming business. But critics say the glamorized picture peddled on social media is misleading and harmful. Viewers see the cute appearance of these animals but not the difficult realities of pet ownership, which can include biting and

Cute photos of small mammals do not show what it is like to live with the animal. People who purchase an animal based on photos are often unprepared to keep it.

Marmosets need a tropical habitat to live in, and they need to live with other marmosets. This makes them difficult pets for many people.

aggressive behavior, messes to clean up, and damaged furniture. And all too often, also hidden from view are the unpleasant realities behind the industry supplying these pets.

NOT DOMESTICATED

Some pets, such as sugar gliders and prairie dogs, can be bred in captivity. However, they are still wild, undomesticated animals, and wild animals do not make good pets for most people. They are more likely to bite or scratch out of fear or aggression. They have not undergone the long history of domestication that other pets have gone through. Even when they are bred in

captivity, they still retain many of their wild instincts. As a
result, these animals are not as well adapted to living
in people's homes. Living in captivity can cause them
great stress. In addition, they often have very complex,
specific needs that are hard to provide for in an ordinary
household. Because they are challenging to take care of,
many end up neglected or abandoned.

For these reasons, some animal advocates warn
against keeping pet sugar gliders, prairie dogs, and other
exotic animals that are not fully domesticated. Weitzman
says, "Just because we can make them our pets doesn't
necessarily make it right to do so."[3] Others argue that
these animals can be good pets as long as they are
properly socialized and given the right care. Michelle
Navarino, who lives with 19 prairie dogs, says the animals
are complex and demanding but can make affectionate
companions under the right circumstances. She rescues
prairie dogs abandoned by pet owners who decided
they were too hard to care for. "I just ask people to do the
research," she says.[4]

WILDLIFE TRAFFICKING

Another controversial issue in small pet ownership is pets
captured from the wild. Between 2000 and 2014, the
United States imported 3.24 billion live animals. About half
of those animals came from the wild.[5] Wild animals are

captured and sold for various purposes, including food, clothing, medicine, and jewelry. Many of these are caught and sold for the pet trade.

Some of these animals are sustainably bred in captivity and legally sold. However, many popular exotic species are wild animals poached from their natural habitat and traded illegally. In fact, according to the US State Department, wildlife trafficking is the third-biggest category of illegal trade after drugs and weapons. It's a vast, global industry that brings in up to $20 billion a year.[6]

While there are local, national, and international laws in place regulating the trade of wild animals, they often go unenforced. That's especially true online, where transactions are hard to track or control. Some sellers pass off wild animals as captive bred to get around laws protecting these species, misleading buyers. Many of the animals being sold are considered threatened or endangered in the wild.

In particular, social media platforms such as Facebook are a hotbed for illegal trade. A 2016 study of Facebook groups selling wildlife from Malaysia found that 86 percent of the species being sold were illegal under CITES. Similarly, the World Wildlife Fund studied Facebook ads selling wildlife from Myanmar and found that 71 percent of the species were protected by law. Eighty-seven percent were captured in the wild.[7]

Conservation groups are working with social media services such as Facebook, Instagram, TikTok, and others to try to curb online wildlife trafficking. These sites now ban certain ads and filter out certain key words. Since 2018, more than 11 million posts advertising illegal wildlife worldwide have been blocked or taken down.[8] However, experts say it's still too easy for sellers to find ways to get around these restrictions. "It isn't easy to fight a billion-dollar industry," says Melissa Kaplan, an environmental educator in Northern California. "As long as there are people to buy, exotic animal dealers will cheerfully sell, no matter what the impact is on wild populations or on the animals."[9]

Trafficked animals are often kept in unsanitary and cramped conditions.

DEADLY CONSEQUENCES

For some small mammal species, such as slow lorises, the consequences of the pet trade have been devastating. Slow lorises are a group of eight species of nocturnal primates native to Southeast Asia. They are the world's only venomous primate, with venom glands in their arms that they lick when threatened to deliver a venomous bite.

In the wild, their numbers are quickly dwindling because of deforestation and habitat loss. All species are now considered vulnerable, endangered, or critically endangered. Although they are protected by both local and international laws, thousands of slow lorises are poached from the wild every year and illegally sold. Large numbers of them are captured for the pet trade. In fact, experts consider the pet trade to be one of the greatest threats to the survival of slow lorises in the wild.

A THREAT TO BIODIVERSITY

Experts say wildlife trafficking is the second-greatest threat to global biodiversity after habitat destruction. Many species are in danger of extinction because they are being traded internationally, including for the pet trade. "We shouldn't allow for every animal that fits into a cage or glass tank to be kept as a pet," says Sandra Altherr, cofounder of the German conservation organization Pro Wildlife.[10] She says that governments should allow ownership only of species with scientific evidence that they can be safely transported and kept.

A worker releases a slow loris that was rescued from illegal trade into a forest on the island of Java.

Viral videos on YouTube have helped feed the demand for slow loris pets, according to Anna Nekaris, who studies primates at Oxford Brookes University in the United Kingdom. Their cute furry faces and big eyes have won the small animals an online fan following. For example, one video of a slow loris eating a rice ball has more than 14 million views on YouTube.[11] Although many say their pets were bred in captivity, Nekaris says that's unlikely. Slow lorises are so difficult to breed in captivity that even experts in zoos struggle to have successful matings. That means most slow lorises being sold have come straight from the wild.

Before selling them as pets, vendors cut out the lorises' front teeth, often without anesthesia. That's to protect pet owners from their toxic bite. In the process, many suffer infections, and some die. Others die during transit, shipped in poorly ventilated crates. Those that survive the ordeal often experience stressful conditions as household pets. In a 2016 study, Nekaris and fellow researchers at Oxford Brookes University watched 100 online videos of pet lorises.[12] Each one showed signs of stress, illness, or exposure to unhealthy conditions.

CRUELTY IN CAPTIVITY

The harsh conditions slow lorises face as part of the international pet trade are not limited to animals that are illegally trafficked. Many animals bred in captivity or legally obtained also endure terrible conditions at every stage, from breeding to selling. Many exotic pets are sold to owners who are not prepared to take care of their needs. For example, because they are so challenging to care for, only 10 to 15 percent of kinkajous stay in the homes they start out in.[14] But many more die before they even have a chance to be sold.

Wild-caught animals in particular that are traded in the global pet industry are shipped long distances under stressful conditions. As a result, many die in transit or soon after. Those that survive shipment are sometimes kept by wholesalers in substandard conditions until they are sold.

CHAPTER 8

MORE THAN CUTE AND CUDDLY

ocial media sites often glamorize exotic, rare wildlife and misrepresent pets as easier to care for than they really are. The internet has also made it easier for the illegal pet trade to flourish. This has harmful repercussions for both animals in the wild and for pets. At the same time, however, social media and the internet have had some positive effects.

Thanks to the internet, it is easier than ever to become educated about animal welfare and to find information about how to responsibly care for a small mammal. It is also easier than ever to connect with advocacy organizations and to find communities devoted to promoting the interests of these complicated animals. And while social media sites can spread misinformation, they can also offer a unique opportunity

People who take the time to learn about how to best care for their pet will be able to form close bonds with their animals.

for education. For example, Alexandra Ashe, founder of a sanctuary for kinkajous, uses her TikTok platform to educate her 2.5 million followers about how difficult it is to care for the exotic animals in captivity.[1]

International Animal Rescue, an animal protection and conservation organization, mounted an online campaign to raise awareness about the plight of slow lorises. It called its campaign "Tickling Is Torture" to counter viral videos of slow lorises being tickled, which often causes the animals to appear to smile. However, experts say that this facial expression is a sign of stress, not pleasure. Georgia Moloney of the University of Adelaide in Australia says the successful campaign "demonstrates the power of social media and the role it can play in preventing animal cruelty and exploitation."[2]

CHANGING ATTITUDES

Scientific understanding of animal welfare has evolved greatly in recent years. Experts now know that small mammals are much more complex than once thought. They form social relationships, engage in play, interact with their environments, and exercise cognitive skills such as problem-solving. To stay physically and mentally healthy, small mammals need opportunities to exercise all these capacities. Pets confined to a small space without sufficient stimulation suffer from stress, boredom, and

People who love a certain species can get involved in rescue or with a sanctuary rather than buying a pet.

poor health. Social species that are deprived of interaction become depressed.

As a result of this evolving knowledge, people's perceptions of pet ownership are also changing. A greater number of pet owners are more invested in their small mammals' care. "Customers are doing their research and they're becoming more educated, which is good because that keeps animals healthier and happier," says Mike Hresko, who owns a pet store in Maryland.[3]

Customers are showing a growing interest in the nutritional needs of their small mammal pets. Many are also increasingly interested in learning about other ways to improve their small pets' lives. That includes providing a

Many small mammals can be taught tricks.

big enough living space. It also includes providing plenty of opportunities for exercise, exploration, stimulation, and enrichment. For example, scattering food in their bedding gives small rodents an opportunity to forage and dig. Toys, including simple homemade cardboard tubes and boxes or wooden blocks for chewing, allow small mammals to exercise their motor skills and coordination as well as engage in natural behaviors such as gnawing, climbing, and perching. Hiding treats in tubes or mazes encourages them to use problem-solving skills. Owners can also train their pets. Some rabbits and guinea pigs have even achieved trick championships through Do More With Your Dog!, a website that allows owners of any species to submit a video of their animal doing certain tricks for judging.

A NATURAL CONNECTION

For those able to make the commitment, caring for a pet can be a wonderful experience. Pets are an important source of comfort, companionship, and connection. That's true of small mammal pets too. "We are naturally drawn to animals, whether it's a rat or a cat or a Great Dane," says veterinarian Chris Miller. "It's something that is healthy and good for people, animals, and the community."[4]

Michelle Gross can attest to that natural connection. She got her pet chinchilla Phil E. Chinchilla when she was going through a difficult time and needed positivity and support. "I saw Phil and knew that he would be that support for me," she says. People don't expect a chinchilla to have the same emotional attachment as a dog or a cat, Gross explains, but she enjoys a strong bond with Phil. "If I'm having a hard day he'll actually spend more time with me,

LEARNING RESPONSIBILITY

Dominique Cahill's two guinea pigs, Peanut and Pumpkin, amuse her with their funny antics. "Peanut jumps like a popcorn kernel popping when he is happy. Pumpkin likes to sit on top of his house and whistle when I bring him lettuce," says the Los Angeles resident. She says the two pets are a great stress reliever, and they have also helped her grow as a person. "They taught me it is hard to be responsible for something so vulnerable. They also entertain me when I am feeling down or stressed out and just need some cuddles."[5]

he'll actually spend more time sitting on my shoulder and cuddling up to me."[6]

Pets provide value and enjoyment to many people. For those experiencing anxiety or depression, caring for a pet can be a lifesaver. After her son got ill and died at age 30, Sharon Hawker-Baddeley struggled with her mental health. Her doctor suggested a pet could help her cope with her grief. She opted for a pair of rabbits and says the two animals have been a source of comfort. "It's very difficult to be miserable around such adorable creatures," she says. "As long as the person can provide what the pet needs, I'd recommend it. It really helps having something to form a bond with."[7]

For Nina Hohimer, a domestic abuse survivor, taking care of pet rats has been a way to cope with trauma. "Recovery from trauma is a long road, and I would say that it is certainly easier with these little guys helping us," she says. "The rats have

Feeding a small mammal treats by hand can help the animal bond with a person.

helped me and my girls cope with a lot of emotional and psychological healing. The [rats] snuggle under our chins when we have flashbacks, anxiety issues or when we are feeling particularly sad. They help a lot with rebuilding our confidence and with quieting our nerves."[9]

THERAPEUTIC PETS

The benefits of spending time with an animal go far beyond comfort and companionship, however. Recent studies indicate that spending time with a pet brings a host of health benefits, from lower levels of stress to reduced blood pressure and reduced risk of heart disease. Therapy with animals has been shown to help in a range of conditions, from Alzheimer's disease to autism. For example, one recent study showed that when children

PET THERAPY

with autism spectrum disorders played with guinea pigs, they became less anxious and showed more interactive social behavior.

Pets can even help in the classroom. Abby Chesnut has visited schools around the country with her therapy rat Oliver, helping struggling readers. Oliver sits near the children while they read, reducing their stress levels. Chesnut says she's seen a big improvement in some of the kids she's worked with. "At first, they were uneasy and stumbled their words, and now they are reading faster and clearer with confidence to boot."[10] Chesnut has also brought Oliver to therapy sessions with stressed-out college students. And she maintains a blog, Healing Whiskers, with information for other people interested in training their pet rats to be therapy animals.

Sarah Garone discovered the rewards of caring for a small mammal by accident. She never thought she liked animals and never wanted to own one. But when a friend asked her to pet-sit a rabbit, she reluctantly agreed. Garone soon found herself smitten. And when the owner became unable to take the rabbit back, she jumped at the chance to adopt him permanently. Doting on her cherished pet has enriched her life, she says, especially during the isolation of the COVID-19 lockdown. "With Nibbles's warmth and softness sidled up to me, I feel a little less alone," she says. Her love for Nibbles has also opened her eyes to how important the human-animal connection can be. "In the end, maybe my trouble with animals was simply that I hadn't met the right one," she says.[12]

Small mammals can bring their owners joy.

OWNING A SMALL MAMMAL

Small mammals are cute, sensitive pets that need gentle handling. It takes time and patience to form a bond with them.

DIET: Nutritional needs vary by species, but many small mammal pets eat a primarily plant-based diet that can include vegetables, hay, specially formulated pellets, fruit, or seeds. Ferrets are an exception. These carnivores need a meat-based diet.

SPACE: Small mammals need plenty of space to move around as well as room for a nesting area and for toys, food, and water. For even the tiniest small mammals, the bigger the cage, the better.

ROUTINE CARE: Small mammals need fresh and balanced nutrition. Their cages should be cleaned regularly, and they need regular health checkups.

ENRICHMENT: To stay healthy, small mammals need plenty of exercise, interaction, and stimulation, including regular time outside their cages. Many species are very social and need to be kept in pairs or groups. Some, like hamsters, are solitary creatures that do best alone.

KEY SPECIES

- Gentle and easy to train, rabbits make good companions and need a lot of interaction and time outside their enclosures.
- Available in a range of colors and coat types, guinea pigs are more vocal than most small mammals, communicating with a variety of squeaks and squeals.
- Mice are quiet, tiny rodents that are relatively easy to take care of and love running on their exercise wheels.
- Although considered pests in the wild, rats make friendly, affectionate pets that emotionally bond with their owners.
- Hamsters are entertaining to watch as they run, burrow, and explore, but many prefer not to be handled much.
- Gerbils come from desert habitats and produce very little urine, which makes it easy to clean their living spaces.
- Ferrets are curious, social animals that love interaction and training.
- Native to South America, chinchillas are known for their luxurious fur and have a longer life span than most small mammals, averaging 12 to 15 years.
- Hedgehogs are a popular pet choice among people who have fur allergies.

camaraderie

A feeling of friendliness and togetherness.

colonize

To take over an area of land by sending people to settle that land.

convention

A formal agreement among nations on a matter of shared concern.

enrichment

The act or process of making life richer by adding or increasing desirable things.

exotic

A living thing not native to the place where it is living.

gland

A tissue or organ that secretes a substance.

hormone

A regulatory substance that sparks an action, such as growth, digestion, or sexual maturation, in a tissue or organ.

hybrid

A plant or animal produced from two different types of plant or animal.

incisor

One of the teeth at the front of the mouth that cuts food.

insectivore

An animal that eats insects for food.

invasive species

An organism that arrives in a new ecosystem, takes over, and causes harm.

marsupial

A mammal that typically has a pouch in which to carry and nurse young.

microorganism

A living thing too small to be seen with the naked eye.

municipality

A primary urban political unit, usually with powers of self-government.

tortoiseshell

A color pattern consisting of patches of white, black, and brown or orange fur.

zoonotic

Spread from animals to humans.

SELECTED BIBLIOGRAPHY

Boriss, Jill. "Facts about Small Mammals as Pets." *Petfinder*, n.d., petfinder.com. Accessed 30 Nov. 2022.

Francis, Richard C. *Domesticated: Evolution in a Man-Made World*. W. W. Norton & Co., 2015.

Gamillo, Elizabeth. "Why Your Pet Rabbit Is More Docile than Its Wild Relative." *Science*, 25 June 2018, science.org. Accessed 1 Dec. 2022.

FURTHER READINGS

Alderton, David. *The Complete Practical Guide to Small Pets and Pet Care*. Lorenz, 2021.

Idzikowski, Lisa. *Ethical Pet Ownership: Puppy Mills, Rescue Pets, and Exotic Animal Trade*. Greenhaven, 2019.

Müller, Isabel. *Clicker Training for Rabbits, Guinea Pigs, and Other Small Pets*. Fox Chapel, 2023.

ONLINE RESOURCES

To learn more about small mammals as pets, please visit **abdobooklinks.com** or scan this QR code. These links are routinely monitored and updated to provide the most current information available

For more information on this subject, contact or visit the following organizations:

American Fancy Rat and Mouse Association

PO Box 2589
Winnetka, CA 91396
afrma.org

Founded in 1983, the American Fancy Rat and Mouse Association promotes the breeding and exhibition of fancy rats and mice and provides information about caring for them.

American Ferret Association

PO Box 554
Frederick, MD 21705
afa@ferret.org
ferret.org

The American Ferret Association's mission is to educate the public about pet ferrets, fight against anti-ferret legislation and mistreatment of ferrets, and provide information and resources for owners, including resources on veterinarians and rescue shelters.

House Rabbit Society

148 Broadway
Richmond, CA 94804
rabbit-center@rabbit.org
rabbit.org

An international nonprofit organization dedicated to rescuing abandoned rabbits, the House Rabbit Society also works to educate people about properly caring for companion rabbits and to promote responsible pet ownership.

CHAPTER 1. SMALL MAMMALS AS PETS

1. "Pet Industry Market Size, Trends & Ownership Statistics." *American Pet Products Association*, n.d., americanpetproducts.org. Accessed 16 Feb. 2023.

2. David Alderton. *The Complete Practical Guide to Small Pets and Pet Care*. Lorenz, 2021. 84.

3. Guy Musser. "Guinea Pig." *Encyclopedia Britannica*, 5 Jan. 2023, britannica.com. Accessed 16 Feb. 2023.

4. Lianne McLeod. "How to Care for a Pet Mouse." *Spruce Pets*, 22 Dec. 2021, thesprucepets.com. Accessed 16 Feb. 2023.

5. "Ferret Facts." *Mammal Facts*, n.d., mammalfacts.com. Accessed 16 Feb. 2023.

6. Joseph F. Merritt. *The Biology of Small Mammals*. Johns Hopkins University Press, 2010. 1.

7. Amy the Bunny Lady. "How Big Do Rabbits Get? (Smallest and Largest Breeds)." *Bunny Lady*, n.d., bunnylady.com. Accessed 16 Feb. 2023.

8. Connie Isbell and Audrey Pavia. *Rabbits for Dummies*. John Wiley & Sons, 2020. 34.

9. Teri Karush Rogers. "The UnDog and the NonCat." *New York Times*, 26 Dec. 2008, nytimes.com. Accessed 16 Feb. 2023.

10. Kim Mueller. "They're Intelligent and Friendly. Why Some People Think Rats Are the Perfect Pet, for Fun and Comfort." *Washington Post*, 5 Oct. 2019, washingtonpost.com. Accessed 16 Feb. 2023.

CHAPTER 2. FROM WILD TO HOUSE PETS

1. Andrew T. Smith. "Rabbit." *Encyclopedia Britannica*, 29 Mar. 2021, britannica.com. Accessed 16 Feb. 2023.

2. Connie Isbell and Audrey Pavia. *Rabbits for Dummies*. John Wiley & Sons, 2020. 33.

3. Ángela Vergara. "From Wilderness to Breeding Farms: The Domestication of the *Chinchilla Lanigera*." *Environment & Society Portal*, Autumn 2022, environmentandsociety.org. Accessed 16 Feb. 2023.

4. Kim Mueller. "They're Intelligent and Friendly. Why Some People Think Rats Are the Perfect Pet, for Fun and Comfort." *Washington Post*, 5 Oct. 2019, washingtonpost.com. Accessed 16 Feb. 2023.

CHAPTER 3. CHOOSING A PET

1. Mari-Jane Williams. "Choosing the Best Pet for Your Family." *Washington Post*, 8 Oct. 2014, washingtonpost.com. Accessed 16 Feb. 2023.

2. David Alderton. *The Complete Practical Guide to Small Pets and Pet Care*. Lorenz, 2021. 31.

3. "Ferret Lifespan." *Ferret World*, n.d., ferret-world.com. Accessed 16 Feb. 2023.

4. Connie Isbell and Audrey Pavia. *Rabbits for Dummies*. John Wiley & Sons, 2020. 74.

5. Alderton, *Complete Practical Guide*, 77.

6. Robin Micheli. "Exotic Pets: A Growing American Fad." *CNBC*, 13 Feb. 2014, cnbc.com. Accessed 16 Feb. 2023.

7. Lauren Barbato. "Hedgehogs = Best Pets Ever?" *Bustle*, 2 June 2014, bustle.com. Accessed 16 Feb. 2023.

8. Amy the Bunny Lady. "When Should You Consider Getting a Second Pet Rabbit?" *Bunny Lady*, n.d., bunnylady.com. Accessed 16 Feb. 2023.

9. Alderton, *Complete Practical Guide*, 83.

10. "Hamster Temperature: Guide to Keeping Your Pet Warm." *Hamsteropedia*, n.d., hamsteropedia.com. Accessed 16 Feb. 2023.

11. Natasha Daly. "Here's Why Easter Is Bad for Bunnies." *National Geographic*, 11 Apr. 2017, nationalgeographic.com. Accessed 16 Feb. 2023.

12. Suzanne S. Summers. "So You Think You'd Like to Have a Rabbit in the House." *Washington Post*, 21 Apr. 2000, washingtonpost.com. Accessed 16 Feb. 2023.

13. Katie Honan. "The Trouble with Guinea Pigs: Council Sitting on Bill to Ban Sales of Fluffy Rodents as Pets." *City*, 13 Sept. 2022, thecity.nyc. Accessed 16 Feb. 2023.

CHAPTER 4. SMALL MAMMAL CARE

1. Melanie D. G. Kaplan. "Teen Hopes to Find 'Forever Homes' for Pint-Sized Pets." *Washington Post*, 13 Apr. 2021, washingtonpost.com. Accessed 16 Feb. 2023.

2. Gregory Rich. "Hedgehogs—Feeding." *VCA Animal Hospitals*, n.d., vcahospitals.com. Accessed 16 Feb. 2023.

3. "Take a Trip on the Wild Side: Ethical Exotic Pet Ownership." *Texas A&M University School of Veterinary Medicine & Biomedical Sciences*, 9 Apr. 2021, vetmed.tamu.edu. Accessed 16 Feb. 2023.

4. Mari-Jane Williams. "Choosing the Best Pet for Your Family." *Washington Post*, 8 Oct. 2014, washingtonpost.com. Accessed 16 Feb. 2023.

5. Connie Isbell and Audrey Pavia. *Rabbits for Dummies*. John Wiley & Sons, 2020. 82.

6. Gary Weitzman. *Complete Guide to Pet Health, Behavior, and Happiness*. National Geographic, 2019. 107.

7. Sarah Armstrong. "Five Reasons Why Rats Make the Best Pets." *BCTV*, 3 Apr. 2021, bctv.org. Accessed 16 Feb. 2023.

8. Weitzman, *Complete Guide*, 107.

9. Gregory Rich and Rick Axelson. "Ferrets—Housing." *VCA Animal Hospitals*, n.d., vcahospitals.com. Accessed 16 Feb. 2023.

10. Sadie Dingfelder. "It's Illegal to Own a Ferret in DC, but 'Fur Baby' Love Transcends Law." *Washington Post*, 9 Mar. 2015, washingtonpost.com. Accessed 16 Feb. 2023.

CHAPTER 5. INDUSTRY AND COMMUNITY

1. "Pet Mouse Guide: What You Need to Know." *A-Z Animals*, 5 Apr. 2022, a-z-animals.com. Accessed 16 Feb. 2023.

2. Sarah Armstrong. "Five Reasons Why Rats Make the Best Pets." *BCTV*, 3 Apr. 2021, bctv.org. Accessed 16 Feb. 2023.

3. Mari-Jane Williams. "Choosing the Best Pet for Your Family." *Washington Post*, 8 Oct. 2014, washingtonpost.com. Accessed 16 Feb. 2023.

4. Dan Gunderson. "Minnesota Rabbit Rescue Group Operator Charged with Animal Cruelty." *MPR News*, 6 July 2022, mprnews.org. Accessed 16 Feb. 2023.

5. Natasha Daly. "Here's Why Easter Is Bad for Bunnies." *National Geographic*, 11 Apr. 2017, nationalgeographic.com. Accessed 16 Feb. 2023.

6. "Hong Kong Population 2023 (Live)." *World Population Review*, n.d., worldpopulationreview.com. Accessed 16 Feb. 2023.

7. Adrienne Kruzer. "How Much Does a Pet Rabbit Cost to Care For?" *Spruce Pets*, 17 June 2021, thesprucepets.com. Accessed 16 Feb. 2023.

8. "Small Animal Cages." *Chewy*, n.d., chewy.com. Accessed 16 Feb. 2023.

9. Abi Cushman. "How Much Does a Pet Rabbit Cost?" *My House Rabbit*, n.d., myhouserabbit.com. Accessed 16 Feb. 2023.

10. "How Much Does a Hamster Cost?" *PetMD*, 1 Mar. 2016, petmd.com. Accessed 16 Feb. 2023.

11. Suzanne S. Summers. "So You Think You'd Like to Have a Rabbit in the House." *Washington Post*, 21 Apr. 2000, washingtonpost.com. Accessed 16 Feb. 2023.

12. Nicole. "How Much Does a Hamster Cost? (Including Care Costs)." *Hamsters101.com*, 19 Nov. 2018, hamsters101.com. Accessed 16 Feb. 2023.

13. "Yearly Cost of Owning a Ferret." *BeChewy*, 14 Dec. 2015, be.chewy.com. Accessed 16 Feb. 2023.

14. Armstrong, "Rats Make the Best Pets."

15. Brian J. Lowney. "Guinea Pigs Make Great Starter Pets." *SouthCoastToday: Standard-Times*, 19 Apr. 2015, southcoasttoday.com. Accessed 16 Feb. 2023.

16. "Beauty Isn't Everything at Annual Gerbil Pageant." *Washington Post*, 6 May 2013, washingtonpost.com. Accessed 16 Feb. 2023.

CHAPTER 6. REGULATIONS

1. Kathleen Conti. "Cambridge Bans Retail Sales of Commercially Bred Pets." *Boston Globe*, 8 Aug. 2017, bostonglobe.com. Accessed 16 Feb. 2023.

2. Conti, "Cambridge Bans Retail Sales."

3. Özgün Emre Can, Neil D'Cruze, and David W. Macdonald. "Dealing in Deadly Pathogens: Taking Stock of the Legal Trade in Live Wildlife and Potential Risks to Human Health." *Global Ecology and Conservation*, vol. 17, Jan. 2019, sciencedirect.com. Accessed 16 Feb. 2023.

4. Andrew J. Campa. "One Man Is Fighting to End California's Ban on Ferrets. Is Time Running Out?" *Los Angeles Times*, 24 June 2022, latimes.com. Accessed 16 Feb. 2023.

5. Sadie Dingfelder. "It's Illegal to Own a Ferret in DC, but 'Fur Baby' Love Transcends Law." *Washington Post*, 9 Mar. 2015, washingtonpost.com. Accessed 16 Feb. 2023.

6. Campa, "California's Ban on Ferrets."

7. "Laws That Protect Animals: Federal, State, & Local." *Animal Legal Defense Fund*, n.d., aldf.org. Accessed 16 Feb. 2023.

8. Dalia Faheid. "The Newest TikTok Stars Are Exotic Pets, but Experts Say That's a Problem." *NPR*, 4 July 2021, npr.org. Accessed 16 Feb. 2023.

9. Lisa Gutierrez. "How Kansas, Missouri and Prairie Dogs Were Involved in First US Outbreak of Monkeypox." *Kansas City Star*, 19 June 2022, kansascity.com. Accessed 16 Feb. 2023.

CHAPTER 7. PET DEBATES

1. Roseandwinston. "Roseandwinston." *TikTok*, n.d., tiktok.com. Accessed 16 Feb. 2023.

2. Maya the Fennec Fox. "Mayafennecfox." *Instagram*, n.d., instagram.com. Accessed 16 Feb. 2023.

3. Gary Weitzman. *Complete Guide to Pet Health, Behavior, and Happiness*. National Geographic, 2019. 24.

4. Claudia Puente. "Lubbock Prairie Dog Rescue Asks for People to Do Research before Adopting." *EverythingLubbock.com*, 2 Aug. 2022, everythinglubbock.com. Accessed 16 Feb. 2023.

5. Rachel Nuwer. "Many Exotic Pets Suffer or Die in Transit, and Beyond— and the US Government Is Failing to Act." *National Geographic*, 2 Mar. 2021, nationalgeographic.com. Accessed 16 Feb. 2023.

6. K. M. Smith et al. "Summarizing US Wildlife Trade with an Eye toward Assessing the Risk of Infectious Disease Introduction." *EcoHealth*, vol. 14, 2017, pp. 29–39, link.springer.com. Accessed 16 Feb. 2023.

7. "Detailed Discussion of the Exotic Pet Trade." *Michigan State University Animal Legal & Historical Center*, n.d., animallaw.info. Accessed 16 Feb. 2023.

8. "Exotic Pet Trade."

9. Don Oldenburg. "Born to Be Wild." *Washington Post*, 30 July 2003, washingtonpost.com. Accessed 16 Feb. 2023.

10. Nuwer, "Many Exotic Pets Suffer or Die."

11. "Slow Loris Eating a Rice Ball." *YouTube*, uploaded by SlowLorisChannel, 12 Aug. 2021, youtube.com.

12. Annie Roth. "Don't Be Fooled by Social Media—Wild Animals Make Terrible Pets." *National Geographic*, 30 Jan. 2019, nationalgeographic.com. Accessed 16 Feb. 2023.

13. Jani Hall. "Wild Otters Are the Latest Exotic Pet Trend." *National Geographic*, 10 Jan. 2019, nationalgeographic.com. Accessed 16 Feb. 2023.

14. Dalia Faheid. "The Newest TikTok Stars Are Exotic Pets, but Experts Say That's a Problem." *NPR*, 4 July 2021, npr.org. Accessed 16 Feb. 2023.

CHAPTER 8. MORE THAN CUTE AND CUDDLY

1. Kinkatopia. "Kinkatopia." *TikTok*, n.d., tiktok.com. Accessed 16 Feb. 2023.

2. "Video Platforms Normalize Exotic Pets." *ScienceDaily*, 28 May 2021, sciencedaily.com. Accessed 16 Feb. 2023.

3. Ethan D. Mizer. "Small-Animal Food Trends Turn Premium." *Pet Product News*, 1 May 2021, petproductnews.com. Accessed 16 Feb. 2023.

4. Mari-Jane Williams. "Choosing the Best Pet for Your Family." *Washington Post*, 8 Oct. 2014, washingtonpost.com. Accessed 16 Feb. 2023.

5. "Features: Meet the Pets Ruling the Lives of These LA-Based Models." *Models NEWfaces*, 18 Mar. 2019, models.com. Accessed 16 Feb. 2023.

6. Jordan Walker, Lolia Briggs, and Alexandra Katsoulis. "This Chinchilla Saw a Couple through Tough Times." *In the Know*, 4 Oct. 2022, intheknow.com. Accessed 16 Feb. 2023.

7. Catherine Mackinlay. "'Rabbit Version of Crazy Cat Lady' Decorates 60ft Enclosure for Christmas as Pets Help Her Cope with Son's Death." *Hull Live,* 26 Oct. 2022, hulldailymail.co.uk. Accessed 16 Feb. 2023.

8. Katharine Zarrella. "Happy and Healthy." *Vogue*, 14 July 2010, vogue.com. Accessed 16 Feb. 2023.

9. Kim Mueller. "They're Intelligent and Friendly. Why Some People Think Rats Are the Perfect Pet, for Fun and Comfort." *Washington Post*, 5 Oct. 2019, washingtonpost.com. Accessed 16 Feb. 2023.

10. Ellen Scott. "Vincent the Therapy Rat Travels to Schools and Libraries to Help Children Learn to Read." *Metro*, 21 May 2019, metro.co.uk. Accessed 16 Feb. 2023.

11. Niki Vettel. "A Small but Powerful Interaction." *Pet Partners*, n.d., petpartners.org. Accessed 16 Feb. 2023.

12. Sarah Garone. "I Never Liked Animals. Then I Got a Pandemic Pet Bunny." *Washington Post*, 2 Apr. 2021, washingtonpost.com. Accessed 16 Feb. 2023.

ABOUT THE AUTHOR

Elisabeth Herschbach lives in Maryland, where she works as an editor and writer. She has written more than a dozen nonfiction books for K–12 readers.